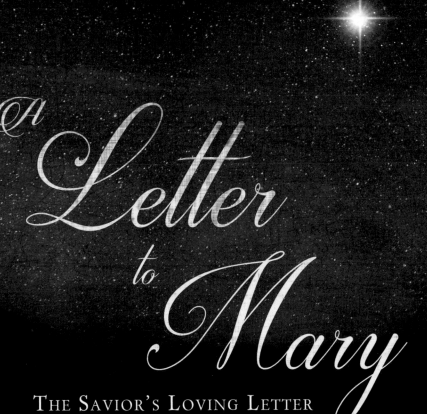

A Letter to Mary

THE SAVIOR'S LOVING LETTER
TO HIS MOTHER

ISBN 13: 978-1-4621-1943-1

Published by CFI, an imprint of Cedar Fort, Inc.
2373 W. 700 S., Springville, UT 84663
Distributed by Cedar Fort, Inc., www.cedarfort.com

LIBRARY OF CONGRESS CONTROL NUMBER: 2016942349

Cover and interior design by Kinsey Beckett
Cover design © 2016 Cedar Fort, Inc.
Edited by Rebecca Bird

Printed in the United States of America

10 9 8 7 6 5 4 3 2 1

Printed on acid-free paper

A Letter to Mary

THE SAVIOR'S LOVING LETTER TO HIS MOTHER

JASON AND KODI WRIGHT

CFI
An Imprint of Cedar Fort, Inc.
Springville, Utah

From the Author

Writers say that every book is a labor of love. *A Letter to Mary* is that and so much more. It's about a woman whom I adore, written from the point of view of a man we worship, and created by a team that I love.

I'm grateful for my wife, Kodi Wright, and for her keen eye for truth and beauty. I'm also thankful to the families who provided our locations and wardrobes: the Baldwin, Cottrell, Gagnon, Massey, Peer, and Robinson families.

I'm indebted to Kinsey Beckett of Cedar Fort for her gorgeous design of each and every page and to McKell Parsons for managing the project from the concept to the manuscript to the stunning book you now hold in your hands.

Also, a sincere thanks to the models who brought these divine men and women to life: Jadi Wright as Mary, Spencer

Shemwell as Joseph, Bexley Shemwell as the infant Jesus, Matthew Richards as the boy Jesus, and Rosie Gagnon as Elisabeth. While they may not be precise physical matches of the people they portray, they are precisely as pictured in my mind's eye.

Finally, all thanks go to Jesus Christ, whom we celebrate. I testify that His birth, life, and ministry are real and that His Atonement provides our road home.

Merry Christmas,

Mary,

DID YOU KNOW

you HAVE BEEN ON MY MIND?

More than ever, *songs* and *stories*

bearing your name and fame fill the air.

THEY'RE BEAUTIFUL BITS OF ART;

each invites my SPIRIT

into hearts, minds, chapels, and living rooms.

I KNOW YOU ARE

humbled

BY THE ATTENTION.

BECAUSE YOU NEVER WANTED

this to be about you.

But Mother, in so many ways,

it is all about you.

Mary, I THINK OF YOUR LIFE.

The moment an *angel*

REVEALED THE FATHER'S WILL.

Behold, a virgin shall be with child, and shall bring forth a son

MATTHEW 1:23

You were chosen not by whim,
BUT BY GOD.

YOUR *divine lines*

WERE WRITTEN AND YOUR COURSE SET

long before *Gabriel* appeared.

I THINK OF THOSE three months at Elisabeth's.

Two *friends*. Two *expectant mothers*.

AWARE OF THE OTHER AND THE ROLES THEY WOULD SOON PLAY.

On late nights
YOU STAYED AWAKE
UNDER THE MOONLIGHT
AND *talked*
LIKE SOON-TO-BE MOTHERS.

You *wept* TOGETHER.

Laughed TOGETHER.

Prayed together.

IN THE REVERENCE OF ELISABETH'S HOME, do you remember seeing

the angel Gabriel again?

DO YOU RECALL VISIONS

so sacred

they were not recorded?

Mary,

I THINK OF THAT *silent night.*

You and Joseph

in Bethlehem.

Away from home. So tired.

No room at the inn. Or so you were told.

Your soul, *body,*

and *mind*

KNEW THE TIME HAD COME.

As THE HOUR SLOWLY DREW NEAR,

like a *good friend*

approaching down a long dirt road,

you rejoiced at the *miracle!*

IT FILLED YOU LIKE A WAVE

that grows to a flood

and sweeps the earth.

I THINK OF YOU SWADDLING ME.

The warmth of a *tiny King*

pressing against your neck.

I SEE *Joseph*

touching my face

leaning in

his breath quick

AND HIS *heart on fire.*

You GAZE ON,
INCHES AWAY.

THEN *Joseph*

LOOKS INTO MY EYES

AND SEES NOT HIS OWN,

BUT THE VERY EYES OF *God.*

Mary,

I think of the sky.

Never clearer.

I THINK OF THE MANGER.

never holier.

Glory to God in the highest, and on earth peace, good will toward men

LUKE 2:14

MULTITUDES OF *angels*
watched and rejoiced.

COUNTLESS CHILDREN
OF GOD
still awaiting their grand turn

sang heavenly hosannas.

THEN, LINKED WITH A FATHER ON EARTH

and a Father in heaven,

you raised me.

THOUGH LITTLE WAS WRITTEN OF MY BOYHOOD YEARS,

you and I remember.

I WATCHED JOSEPH
MASTER HIS CRAFT.
He watched me
master mine.

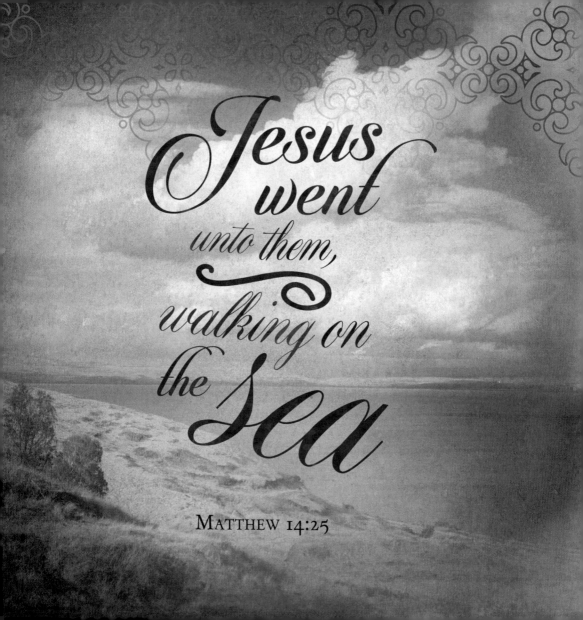

Jesus went unto them, walking on the Sea

MATTHEW 14:25

YOU LEARNED TO WALK WITH ME.

We stood at the edge of the water.

THEN,

YEARS LATER,

I walked on it.

I THOUGHT OF *you*
WHEN I TARRIED
BEHIND IN JERUSALEM.

AND THOUGH I KNEW
I MUST STAY AND BE
ABOUT MY FATHER'S BUSINESS,

MY HEART WAS ALWAYS WITH
you and *Joseph.*

EVEN AS I GREW IN WISDOM AND STATURE,

and in favor with *God* and man,

I REMEMBER THAT

you and *Joseph* worried.

I THINK OF YOUR PRAYERS

to the *Father*

on behalf of your *son*.

I also ponder the *heartache*

that would come.

My pain — unprecedented in history.

You ached, too, in ways
no one has ever known.

You stood alone
as the *mother* of a sinless,
innocent man who was crucified
for all mankind.

You stood for me.

SO MANY FORGET

that I died for *you*, too.

THEY'VE ONLY READ THE STORIES.

You lived them.

Mary, I think of the anguish.

It pains you

HOW THEY TREAT THE

AND *me.*

How the world defames us!

FROM A HOLY MANSION

HIGHER THAN THE HIGHEST CLOUDS,

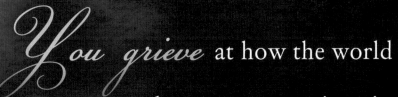 *You grieve* at how the world

shouts my name in vain.

BUT WHEN THE

WORLD RATTLES IN DISBELIEF,

I know my disciples will not give in.

Christians will not deny me.

MY CHRISTIAN FRIENDS

OF ALL FAITHS WILL NEVER STOP TESTIFYING

that I am.

THE SON OF MARY.

As long as I live,
so lives *hope*.

WHAT YOU DID IN THAT

tiny town of Bethlehem

was not for naught.

IT WASN'T TO FILL HISTORY BOOKS

or provide a plot for films,

pages, and stages.

IT WAS AN ACT OF OBEDIENCE,

a miracle,

the beginning of the life
that gave all others life.

EVEN ETERNAL LIFE.

Yes, Mary.

YOU HAVE BEEN ON MY MIND.

May the world know
that without *you*, there is no *Christ*.

WITHOUT CHRIST,

THERE IS NO CHRISTMAS.

LOVE, YOUR SON.

Your Savior

Jason F. Wright is a *New York Times*, *Wall Street Journal*, and *USA Today* bestselling author and a weekly columnist for the *Deseret News* and *Northern Virginia Daily*. He is the author of *Christmas Jars* and *The Wednesday Letters*, among other books. Jason is a popular speaker and has appeared on CNN, Fox News, C-SPAN, and other local television affiliates around the country.

Kodi E. Wright is a wife, mother, and award-winning professional photographer. Her work has appeared on Fox News and TheBlaze.

Jason and Kodi Wright live with their four children in Virginia's Shenandoah Valley. For more information, visit www.jasonfwright.com and www.kodiwrightphotography.com.